When you can

WALK

ON

WATER

Why take the boat?

When you can

WALK

ON

WATER

Why take the boat?

Lisa Diane
Ambassador of Inspiration

**Executive
Books**

When You Can Walk On Water Why Take the Boat?

Published by
Executive Books
206 West Allen Street
Mechanicsburg, PA 17055

Cover design by Terri Depew

ISBN: 0-937539-70-8

LCCN: 2003107761

Printed in the United States of America

Contents

Dedication   *vii*
A Word of Thanks   *ix*
Introduction   *xi*

Dream a Little (or Big) Dream   1
Life Is Not a Box of Chocolates   5
Whether You Think You Can or Think You Can't...   13
When the Prize is Clear, the Price Gets Cheap   15
Goal for It   23
You are What You Think!   29
Accentuate the Positive... Eliminate the Negative!   31
What You Think About You Bring About   37
It's All About Faith   41
The Ancient Formula for Success   47
Step Out of the Boat   57
Your MIRACLE MOMENTS are waiting for you now!   61
Miracle Moments   65
Do You Know the Secret?   69

About the Author   75

Dedication

This book is dedicated to my Dad, without whom I would have never learned the amazing satisfaction and fulfillment in life outside of the boat.

From the time I was a little girl, just old enough to understand, to this day, my father is my biggest fan. He taught me that I could have, be or do absolutely anything in life—and I believed him.

His belief in me was how I learned to believe in myself. His wonderful example of ever enduring love and support as a father taught me to have complete faith and trust in my Heavenly Father.

No one could ask for more—but somehow I got it!

Thanks, Dad. This one is for you!

A Word of Thanks

Every book is a team effort—this book especially so!

Thank you...

Bonnie, without your incredible patience, encouragement and a little "push" from time to time, this book would still be back on my PC. You sacrificed yourself and took on my business responsibilities so that I could concentrate on communicating my message.

To Linda, for being the best mother in the world and for giving up your career—and most of your free time (OK, who am I kidding? What free time??)—to join my mission and play a major role in making a difference in the lives of countless women across the country.

To BJ, for keeping me grounded. You're the best son anyone could ever hope for. I'm so proud of you. You're the best thing I've ever done. I can't wait to have you running my companies and showing people what you're really made of.

To Awie, for being the world's best grandmother and for coming back to work at 76 years young—and having more energy than all the rest combined. Your dedication and commitment are awesome.

To Poppy, for being supportive of the "family" business and not complaining that it's all we ever talk about. While you may not be involved day-to-day, your spirit is a part of me and I love you.

Charlie "Tremendous" Jones. For being the most positive, uplifting, supportive, encourager I've ever known. He's a man who truly walks his talk!

To all the hardworking, optimistic, empowered people at Inspiration Point. We're changing lives... one dream at a time. Thank you for your support.

To Mary Kay Ash, Dave Longaberger, Dr. Wayne Dyer, Dr. Robert Schuller, Charles Givens, Zig Ziglar, Oprah Winfrey, Mark Victor Hansen, Robert Allen, Bill Cosby, Tony Robbins and Randy Gage for providing me with such a wonderful demonstration of life outside the boat. These people prove that ordinary people can indeed live extraordinary lives.

Introduction

Dear Friend,

Do you still have a dream? Dreams are the substance life is made of. Achieving dreams and results in life is not a mystery—it's a process that anyone can learn. Even you! Regardless of your age, inexperience, IQ, education or financial standing, YOU can achieve your dreams. Incredible dreams... wonderful dreams! You can begin to have dreams grander than you have ever had and see them come true right before your very eyes. It's happened for me. Why not for you?

I was a preacher's kid. Growing up, my family didn't have a lot of money, but I was blessed with parents who instilled a deep sense of faith and a belief that I could have or be anything that I wanted to be. Fortunately for me, I believed them.

In my early adult life, I tried my hand at several ventures. I failed at all of them. At one point, I was so broke, I had $50,000 in credit card debt, no income and a feeling of total hopelessness. Have you ever come home to find your car gone? Repossessed while you were out at your child's sporting event. And have you had the bank call telling you to pay them $1,800 in back mortgage payments or they will begin foreclosure proceedings? A few wrong choices and look where I was. Rock bottom.

The sting of poverty hung over me daily. Fear gripped me at night. I would lie in bed and plead with God for direction... for help... for a light to appear at the end of the tunnel.

If only I had known then what I know now. If only the secrets had been revealed a little sooner. If only I had realized how much of my condition I HAD control over and how much I could have done to change my life... right then.

My dear friend, you don't have to live in the land of regrets and 'if only's.' Take my hand. Let me walk with you into the land of extraordinary lives where YOU can start a whole new life-outside the boat.

I look forward to our journey together. So, without further delay, let's begin...

Chapter 1
Dream a Little (Or Big) Dream

There's a very simple formula that allows ordinary people—like you and me—to create extraordinary results in life. Over the last decade of my life I have dedicated myself to discovering the true secret to success. And I'm not talking about just money. Success to me is the ability to live out your biggest dreams each and every day. My journey began at an all-time low point in my life. And although I was blessed to be able to conquer the "financial" problems relatively fast, I've had my moments, my "challenges" over the years. (I still do!) But success truly is a journey—not a destination. There is a formula... a roadmap that you can follow to achieve the success in life that you deserve.

I'd like to share this formula with you and invite you to <u>step out of the boat</u> and experience the thrill of walking on water!

As a Christian I must tell you that it is my sincere belief that you will never experience ultimate satisfaction or achieve your true potential without coming to a personal relationship with Jesus Christ. This book is not about religion. I'm not here to preach to you, however, I would be remiss not to let you know from the beginning that my life and my success are rooted and grounded in my faith and my relationship with Christ. I owe everything in my life to Him.

Jeremiah 29:11 says, *"For I know the plans I have for you says the Lord, plans to prosper you and not harm you, to give you a hope and a future."* If you are a believer, then you should understand that God wants you to have it all! His plans for you are greater than you could ever imagine—even in your wildest dreams!

Over the next few chapters we're going to discuss how YOU can create the life of your dreams. There is nothing in this world that you cannot accomplish if you know the secret. As you read through these pages, stay focused on the message and you will discover the SECRET that will open to you a world full of limitless possibility and absolute abundance in every area of your life.

If you haven't yet created the life of your dreams it isn't because you're not smart enough, it's not because you didn't go to the right school or get the right education, it's not because you weren't "born" into it and it has nothing to do with the color of your skin, how tall or short, fat or thin you may be and it has absolutely nothing to do with "luck" or "chance."

If you're not living the life of your dreams, it's simply because you haven't learned the SECRET. If you're serious about changing your life... if you're ready to put the past behind you and begin experiencing life at its fullest, then you will find what you need within these pages. It's right here waiting for you. Seek and you will find what you're looking for.

I've written this book to share the information that I believe you need to know in order to change your life. I'm going to take you on a journey—not to far off lands but deep inside yourself. Throughout these pages I will ask you to participate with me in a variety of different exercises. Do NOT overlook these, as things will only be revealed to you as you are ready to receive them.

Before we begin I suggest that you find a blank pad of paper or notebook that you can use to complete each exercise that you encounter. These pages will become the blueprint for your immediate action and play a significant role in your ultimate success. Don't put it off. Don't read the book with the idea that you will go back and actually "do" the exercises at some other time. YOU WON'T! Trust me. I've been there and done that (or should I say, NOT done that). Get your notebook and DO IT NOW! Don't pass over a section until you've COMPLETED THE EXERCISE!!!!!!

As the saying goes, "When the student is ready, the teacher will appear." So, if you're ready, let's begin.

Chapter 2
Life Is <u>Not</u> a Box of Chocolates

WHAT THE MIND CAN CONCEIVE AND BELIEVE, IT CAN ACHIEVE.

The first step to having what you want is <u>knowing what you want</u>.

I make it a habit everywhere I go to ask people what they want. It's amazing how few people have an answer. Most people are excellent complainers. They can tell you how unhappy they are, how unfair life is and of course, why none of this is their fault. They're experts at "the blame game" and being victims of their circumstances. But when asked what they WANT in life, the best they can do is tell me what they DON'T want. It never fails. The worse off people are the less idea they have of what they want.

No dreams, no goals and no direction. Most people live their lives at the mercy of others. Whatever happens, happens. This is a very dangerous way to live. Think about it for a moment.

Would you feel comfortable walking into a restaurant knowing that you would be forced to eat whatever food the waiter chose to bring you? Like sushi? How about liver?

Or clothes. What if you could only wear what a salesperson picked out for you? I hear "high water" pants are back in. Or what about tube tops and miniskirts?

Or vacations. What if you had to pack your family- with no idea what kind of climate to pack for- board a plane and get off wherever the airline felt like dropping you? Instead of a week at Walt Disney World, you may end up in spending your week in Chicago in the middle of January.

And while some of these options would be fine for some people, they definitely would not be fine for others. Of course, you would never stand by and allow other people to make those choices for you, right? You decide what kind of food you eat, what clothes you wear and the destination of your family's vacation. Why? Because you know what you want- you have certain expectations to be met.

If we would never allow other people to make small choices for us- like the kind of food we eat- why in the world would we allow them to decide what we get in life? The answer is simple. Most people don't realize they have a choice. Most people were raised being told things like... "don't ask for that... who do you think you are?... that's life... just grin and bear it... it's beyond your control... it's just something you'll have to get used to... because I said so...that's not for people like you... the list goes on and on.

The truth is, life is NOT like a box of chocolates. You CAN know what you will get- IF you will take control and DECIDE what the outcome will be. Are there things that are beyond your control? Absolutely. But how you respond to people, circumstances and events is completely within your control.

The key to having what you want is KNOWING what you want. That's the FIRST STEP to making dreams come true and to living a life of total freedom and abundance.

So, what do you want? When was the last time you thought about that? What DREAMS do you have? What excites you... makes you happy... gives you a sense of satisfaction and fulfillment? Do you know? For many it's been so long since you actually stopped to consider what YOU want in life, it's hard to even know where to begin.

Here's what I want you to do. Right now, before reading any further, I want you to get out a sheet of paper and begin to make a list of all the things you would like to do, have or be in life.

At the top of your paper write the following question:

If I could HAVE, DO or BE absolutely ANYTHING in
life—regardless of time, money or talent—
what would I choose?

Write down anything and everything that you can think of. Don't limit yourself to what you believe you could have or what you think you deserve. Just let your imagination run wild. Don't stop until you have at least 25 dreams on your list. Go ahead, do it now.

(If you'd like a free copy of my personal "dream planner" worksheet you can contact my office at 1-877-462-5448 or visit us online at www.InspirationPoint.net)

I made my first list of dreams back in the early 90s. I listed 25 things I wanted to achieve. <u>I made my list at a time when I had absolutely NOTHING but problems</u>. I had <u>no</u> money, loads of debt, no job and the "light at the end of the tunnel" was growing dimmer by the minute. I was reading a book called *Super Self* by Charles Givens. The book literally transformed my life. (If you can find one in your local book store, BUY IT and read it right away!)

<u>About six months from the day I wrote my original list of 25 dreams, I had achieved 23 of them</u>. And these were no small achievements. My life had a MAJOR turnaround. I had <u>more cash</u> than most people make working full-time for <u>several YEARS</u>, I bought my first Jaguar (my dream car) with CASH, I moved out of a small home that I almost lost to foreclosure and into a 6,000 square foot country club estate and I discovered that there was much more to life than I ever dreamed. Since then I update my DREAMS LIST on a regular basis and continue to be amazed by the results.

You should keep your DREAMS LIST around somewhere that you will see it often. In the beginning, I kept it thumbtacked to the wall right above my desk. Every day when I would sit in my living room at my desk, I would see that list and imagine that those dreams were already a reality. I'd picture myself driving down the road in my dream car (Jaguar) with my favorite jazz music playing and the smell of rich leather all around me. Even though I had lost my car to the repo man, I just knew that my Jaguar was on its way.

Your DREAMS LIST is like a compass. If you look at it everyday and begin imagining what your life is like having accomplished those dreams, you'll be amazed how the direction of your life will begin to move toward those dreams. Until now you've had no real compelling direction in life. You've just drifted here and there—going with the flow. That will all change the moment you begin to use your DREAMS LIST.

Don't delay in doing this exercise. Dreams are the foundation of your life. Without them your life will be directionless. You were created for greatness. You deserve all the richness and abundance that you will accept. God has big plans for you. He wants to give you so much more than you have now. But without a dream, you'll never make a dream come true.

Some people get caught up in the mindset that they don't "deserve" to have all the "extras" in life. They act like owning great cars, homes, having fat bank accounts, being able to travel when and where they want is only for "selfish" or "greedy" people. If that's the way you feel, you need to CHANGE YOUR THINKING right this moment.

There is nothing "righteous" about being poor or living in lack. The Bible continually says that God wants to bless you. Believe me, living under the stress of financial problems or settling for a life of mediocrity is far from what your Heavenly Father wants for you. But He will not violate your free will. You will only get what you expect and what you're willing to receive.

King Solomon was one of richest men who ever lived. He was also a favored man of God. He lived in excess

9

in every area of his life. Throughout the Bible there are examples of the extraordinary blessings that God wants for His children. There are MANY millionaires in the Bible—beginning in Genesis—with people like Abraham, Ishmael, Isaac, Joshua, Jacob and Ruth—to name a few. Abundance and prosperity is your birthright. Anything less is simply not living up to your potential.

I recommend that you make several copies of your DREAMS LIST and post them somewhere that you will see them when you wake up in the morning, before you go to sleep at night, when you're at work, when you're driving in your car, etc. Just make it a part of your daily life.

I want you to think about your DREAMS LIST as a "broad stroke" measure in achieving the success that you desire. This list is a good starting point. It's very important that you take the time to write it down and look at it regularly. But it's only the first step. Now we're going to delve further into the secret of how ordinary people achieve extraordinary results.

Your next step is to begin SEEING your dreams as clearly and detailed as possible. One of the EASIEST and MOST EFFECTIVE ways to do this is to cut out pictures of your dreams and paste them on a large board or frame.

I call it your "DREAM SCENE."

You don't have to spend hours looking for pictures all at once. You can build your Dream Scene over time. Just start looking in magazines you read or advertisements you receive for pictures that best represent your dreams. New cars, fancy homes, exotic trips, happy families, free time, good health—these are all things that you can find in pictures.

Begin working on your DREAM SCENE right away. Soon it will become like a game. You'll automatically begin "spying" your dreams in every book, magazine or advertisement you pick up. **When you find a good picture, CUT IT OUT AND PASTE IT ON YOUR DREAM SCENE.** As time goes on you'll have enough pictures to make multiple DREAM SCENE boards and hang them all around your house or work.

Be sure to place your DREAM SCENE in a place that you will see it often—several times a day. The more you look at it, the more clear your dreams will become.

This may sound silly to you, however, your subconscious mind is looking for suggestions from you. The suggestions you give—either positive or negative—are like commands. It doesn't know the difference between what's "real" and what's "imagined." It also can't determine whether or not something is in your best interest.

Your subconscious mind is simply looking for its "marching orders" from you—its "major general." It will go to work to fulfill your requests—24 hours a day, 7 days a week, 365 days a year. The more positive reinforcement you give it, the more rapidly you will see a change. Having full-color pictures of your dreams (from your Dream Scene) will remind you (both consciously and unconsciously) of the life that you are creating for yourself.

(I'm presently creating a "Dream Scene" Kit that

will include lots of pictures that could be used in creating a Dream Scene—as well as positive words and phrases. For more information contact my office at 1-877-GOAL-4-IT or visit us online at www.InspirationPoint.net.)

Chapter 3
Whether You Think You Can or You Think You Can't... You're Right!

Putting your **DREAMS in writing** (and pictures) is the <u>FIRST STEP</u> to making them happen. It's also one of the most important steps. **The next step is BELIEVING that you CAN have the things you dream—and more.**

      People often ask for the "secret" to my success. They look at my life with envy thinking that I've made it to the "big time" while they're destined to live their lives of struggle and financial turmoil. But I'm no different than anyone else. I wasn't born into money—as a matter of fact, my parents struggled financially my whole life—I didn't win the lottery and I don't have any unique or special skills.

      However, there is ONE major difference between me and my friends who look at my life and wish they could have this kind of success. <u>I decided long ago that getting a job and giving up control of my life was totally out of the question</u>. I HAD to find a way to generate money on my own and I wasn't satisfied with living a life of financial struggle like most people. I wanted more and I believed that I could have it. <u>I cut off all other possibilities for myself—I would settle for NOTHING less than financial success</u>.

I don't mean to sound callous or prideful. That's really not who I am. **I just desperately want YOU to understand the true source of my success.** It's not luck, it's not inherited, it's not skills or education. It's my ATTITUDE. <u>It's my BELIEF that I CAN and WILL achieve whatever I set my mind to do</u>. It's the FAITH that I have that God wants us all to experience the very best of everything in life. We weren't created to live like slaves to a time clock or to spend our days and nights struggling just to pay a few bills. We were destined to have so much more. **Unfortunately, (or fortunately for some of us!) we GET what we EXPECT in life.** And me, I EXPECT more than most people and that's EXACTLY WHAT I GET!

You may be reading this and thinking, *"Yeah, right. It's easy to say these things when you generate more income in a week than many people earn in a year, but what about me?"* You need to know that I put this belief system into action when I wasn't even earning $25 a week. It was this BELIEF SYSTEM that took me from $25 to MORE MONEY than I ever dreamed possible in a very short period of time.

Am I saying that all you need to do is change your thinking and next week you'll be rich next week? Of course not. But I can almost GUARANTEE that if you DON'T change your ATTITUDES and EXPECTATIONS you will NEVER find the success that is well within your reach.

Chapter 4
When the Prize is Clear, the Price Gets Cheap

Each month I write the above quote on my desk calendar. It serves as a great reminder to me. I'll often times use it in strategy meetings with my staff. I believe it contains one of the key ingredients to success in all areas of life. Think about it for a moment.

We've talked about your dreams and the importance of having a DREAMS LIST as an overall compass for your life. Now let's get a little more specific. Let's talk about what you really WANT in life. Unless you are crystal clear on what you want, you will never have the perseverance necessary to "keep on keeping on" when you run up against a challenge or obstacle. If the prize is CLEAR, you will do whatever it takes to achieve it.

Let me give you an example...

Suppose I asked if you could come up with $3,000 in cash for me within the next ten days. I would tell you that the money was for an important cause, but that I couldn't give you the exact details now. And let's also sup-

15

pose that you didn't have an extra $3,000 readily at your fingertips. What would you tell me? If you're like most people you would say that you didn't have the money, end of story.

Now let's suppose your "dream car" is a Mercedes 500SL convertible (selling for $80,000 or more). And let's pretend that I came to see you holding a shiny set of car keys. And once again I asked if you could come up with $3,000 in the next ten days—but this time I told you that if you could, you would receive the keys to this brand new Mercedes convertible. What would your answer be? Of course you could come up with the money. Are you kidding? The chance to own a brand new Mercedes for only $3,000—you would do whatever it took to come up with the money.

What's the difference? In one case you were sure you could not come up with the money and in the other you were positive that you could. What happened? Did your financial picture change in the three seconds between questions?

No, the difference is that the PRIZE suddenly became crystal CLEAR. You knew exactly what you were working for and you were willing to make whatever sacrifices necessary to achieve the end result—your new Mercedes.

The truth is, I have a lot more to offer you than a new Mercedes. If you can truly grasp this concept and develop a clear picture of your "PRIZE," then you can have absolutely ANYTHING and EVERYTHING you want in life. There are NO LIMITS!

When your PRIZE IS CLEAR, the PRICE gets cheap. All of the sacrifices you have to make... the steps you have to take out of your comfort zone... the commitment... the perseverance... it's all worth it. Why? Because you have a clear picture of the "PAY OFF." You know what the END RESULT will bring. Your PRIZE is worth the effort.

So, how you do you develop a crystal CLEAR PICTURE of your PRIZE?

If you've completed the steps outlined in this book thus far, you're well on your way. Your DREAMS LIST provides you with part of the picture. Throughout this book you will discover additional ways to clarify your vision and have a crystal clear picture of your PRIZE.

Knowing what you WANT in life is the first step toward achieving it. It's not enough just to "want" something—you actually have to BELIEVE you can have it and EXPECT to receive it. However, formulating a clear picture is the first step toward creating the life you deserve.

How do you know what you really want? The truth is, you can have, be or do ANYTHING in life that you truly desire. But for some people, determining what they want is not an easy task. How about you? Do you know what you REALLY want—not just "things" like cars, homes, money, vacations, etc. Things are easy. I'm talking about what you want to do with your life... who you want to be... the kind of contribution you want to make—discovering YOUR PURPOSE in life. Do you know?

You need to identify the one major idea that compels you, that draws you to it. If you're like most people, you're

17

all caught up in the drudgery of day-to-day living. You probably don't have the answer on the tip of your tongue. That's OK. We have plenty of time to identify the one main compelling force in your life—also known as your PURPOSE.

To discover your PURPOSE you really need to set aside some time to look deep inside yourself and think about who you are and what you're passionate about.

Think back to several specific times in your life—they can be at any age—when you were doing something that made you really happy. It could have lasted for a day, a week, a year or just a matter of moments. Remember times where you know that you were truly happy and fulfilled by what you were doing.

Once you've identified those events, write them down (try to find three or four separate events). Go ahead and write down what it was that made you happy or fulfilled.

Now look at the list. What do they have in common? You should be able to find a "common thread" running through all three events.

Were you teaching or learning something?
Were you helping people or making a contribution?
Were you solving a problem or being creative?
Were you involved in a more "personal" endeavor with an emphasis on relationships?
Were you taking risks or being adventurous?

Look for the common thread. Being able to identify

it will help you determine what you're passionate about in life. If you can't find it—keep looking—it will eventually surface.

In my own life I have been able to identify that I am truly passionate about **helping people**. I believe my purpose in life is to help as many people as I can discover the secret to living extraordinary lives. I've adopted Zig Ziglar's famous principle,

> *"You can have anything you want in life*
> *if you're willing to help enough other people get what*
> *they want."*

I am happiest and most fulfilled when I am in service to others. Knowing that I can make a difference in people's lives is more exciting to me than any new car or fat bank account will ever be. Sure, the financial rewards are wonderful and I am thankful for them, but my satisfaction in life comes from knowing that I can play a part in changing people's lives.

But that's just me. This may not be your PURPOSE in life. Your purpose may be to set a record for climbing the highest mountain or devising new ways for businesses to operate more efficiently or being a patient and kind kindergarten teacher.

There's a unique plan for each of us. It's up to you to find yours. (If you'd like a free copy of my worksheet on "Discovering Your Purpose" you can contact my office at 1-877-462-5448 or visit us online at www.InspirationPoint.net)

Once you have identified your PURPOSE in life, the

19

next step is to clearly define WHAT YOU WANT. One of the greatest ways I've been able to do that is to describe a specific time or event in my life (in the future) when I have achieved my dreams and goals and am living according to my PURPOSE and passion in life.

Just think for a moment about what your life would look like if you were living according to your PURPOSE. Write down what a day in your life would look like—from the time you wake up to the time you go to sleep. **I call this your VIVID VISION**. Describe everything in great detail—from your clothes, your house, the food you eat, the car you drive to the things that you do and the people you interact with. Pretend like you are a motion picture writer and you're creating a scene from a movie. Be as detailed as you can—complete with smells, sounds, sights and emotions. Keep your DREAMS LIST near by and be sure to incorporate as many of them as you can.

Don't write this out according to what you think is realistic or attainable. This is a no holds barred description of a day in your ULTIMATE DREAM LIFE. The only limits are the ones you place on yourself. The possibilities are endless. Just take your time and let your imagination run wild.

Remember, what your mind can conceive and believe, you can achieve!

Now that you have clearly defined WHAT YOU WANT in life, in as much vivid detail as possible, you are ready to start making it happen. Regardless of what you've written out that you want to achieve—whether it's being the President of the United States, a feature film star, the CEO of a Fortune 500 company or the perfect "Proverbs 31" wife and mother—YOU CAN HAVE IT.

Begin reading your VIVID VISION statement aloud once or twice each day—preferably as you begin and end your day.

One word of caution before we go any further: make sure that this is what YOU REALLY WANT. If you follow my instructions, the "details" that you imagine WILL become reality, so be sure they're what you truly desire. I know it's hard for you to believe what I'm saying, but it's absolutely true.

(Let me give you a personal example. When I began "visioning" a Jaguar automobile I always pictured it in burgundy with doe skin color leather and a sunroof. Can you believe that within a few months I ended up owning TWO Jaguars that were almost identical! BOTH of them were burgundy with doe skin leather and a sun roof. When I realized what had happened I changed the picture in my mind. My third Jag was a black convertible. The moral to this story—be sure that what you imagine is what you really want. You may end up with two!)

There are certain "universal laws" that cannot be changed. They're at work in your life right now, but unfortunately, they work against most people. However, once you understand them you can learn to apply them to create POSITIVE results in every area of your life.

You don't necessarily need to understand all the reasons "why" these things work—just like you don't have to understand how electricity works to turn on a light or how a

21

fax machine works to send and receive a fax. The point is, they DO work. Our world was setup on the foundation of certain immutable laws and principles. Your life is ordered by them every single day—whether you understand, acknowledge or consciously apply them.

My challenge to you is to simply take me at my word with these things and make a commitment to "test" them out on a three month trial basis. Follow the steps exactly as outlined in this book. Believe in the principles that I teach. And see what happens. I guarantee that if you'll follow my lead, you will experience extraordinary results in a matter of a few short weeks. Your life will never be the same!

(I'd love to know your progress and have the opportunity to support you in realizing your dreams. You can fax me your dream list or anything else you'd like to share with me toll-free to 1-800-738-1025.)

Chapter 5

Goal for It

Now that you have a list** of AT LEAST 25 DREAMS and you've created your VIVID VISION of a day in your ULTIMATE DREAM LIFE, your NEXT STEP is to choose a few of your dreams and turn them into **WRITTEN GOALS.**

What you'll want to do is look over your DREAMS LIST and choose three or four of your dreams that you would like to pursue immediately. *When doing so, be sure that they are in alignment with your PURPOSE in life. You can accomplish ANYTHING you set your mind to, so it's important that you accomplish things that will bring you closer to ultimate fulfillment and satisfaction.* **These will be the GOALS on which we begin focusing.**

Write these 3-4 GOALS on a separate list and make several copies—one for your car visor, one for your wallet or purse, one for your bathroom mirror, one for your desk at work, one on your refrigerator and one on your nightstand next to your bed.

The key is to read over that GOALS LIST as often

as possible. **Each morning when you wake up, spend three minutes reading over the list and PICTURING those goals as if they are already accomplished**. Feel yourself in the new home or at the new job or driving the new car. Bring in as much detail as you can.

Success does not happen by CHANCE,
it happens by CHANGE!

The next several months can be the most exciting and pleasurable of your life—if you simply make a commitment to CHANGE and follow through with the ACTION steps that I recommend to you in each chapter of this book.

Our next step will be to focus on achieving the GOALS on your GOALS LIST. If you've followed my instructions, you already have a GOALS LIST containing three or four of your DREAMS that you want to begin accomplishing immediately. **You should be studying your GOALS LIST several times a day and spending at least three minutes each morning picturing yourself already having achieved your goals.**

Our next SUCCESS STEP is to begin taking specific ACTION toward the achievement of your GOALS. To do this we are going to follow a very simple, yet extremely powerful daily activity.

24

This daily exercise has been called the *"$35,000 Idea!"*

Back around the turn of the century, Ivy Lee, a renowned efficiency expert, approached Charles Schwab, who at the time was the president of Bethlehem Steel. Lee said, *"I can increase your people's efficiency—and your sales—if you will allow me to spend just fifteen minutes with each of your executives."*

"How much will it cost me?" the shrewd industrialist asked. *"Nothing,"* Lee replied, *"unless it works. After three months you can send me a check for whatever you feel it's worth to you." "It's a deal,"* Schwab replied.

The following day, Lee met with Schwab's top executives, spending only fifteen minutes with each in order to say, *"I want you to promise me that for the next ninety days, before leaving your office at the end of the day, you will make a list of the six most important things you have to do the next day and number them in order of their importance. Scratch off each item after finishing it, and go on to the next one on your list. If something doesn't get done, put it on the following day's list."*

Each executive promised to follow Lee's instructions for the next ninety days. **Three months later, Schwab studied the results and was so pleased that he sent Lee a check for $35,000.00.** <u>In an era when the average American worker was paid $2.00 for a ten HOUR DAY, this was a HUGE sum of money!</u> Schwab was a man who appreciated value and he figured Lee's advice was a BARGAIN at $35,000.00.

I began using this exact same technique years ago and I can honestly say that I believe it is one of the SMARTEST, MOST EFFECTIVE things I've ever done. *Now it's your turn...*

Each evening before you stop working you need to make a **LIST OF THE <u>SIX</u> MOST IMPORTANT THINGS TO DO** the next day. Then, **<u>prioritize</u>** the **LIST OF SIX** from *<u>most important to least important</u>*. Keep your list with you ALL DAY and work through it one thing after another. **Don't worry if you can't finish everything on the list.** <u>Just take any unfinished items and move them to your list for the NEXT DAY</u>.

Keep in mind when making your list that the items you write down should be <u>ONLY</u> actions that **MOVE YOU TOWARD YOUR GOAL**. <u>Don't write things that are daily actions that have nothing to do with accomplishing your goals</u> (Like reading your email, taking a shower, opening the mail, etc.). **And don't write MORE than six things for any single day**. It's important that you keep "healthy" size lists. If you try and list 101 things you need to do, you'll become overwhelmed and end up doing very little to none of them. I keep my LIST OF SIX in a very small memo book that I can carry with me everywhere. <u>You'll be shocked at how focused you become when you have that list to look at all day</u>. **You'll never waste time again and you'll end each day with a great sense of satisfaction!**

<u>It's IMPORTANT that you follow this activity EVERY DAY</u>. It must become a habit. If you do this every day (at least Monday through Friday) for the next three months, it WILL become a natural part of your daily routine. **Don't overlook or underestimate the *LIFE-***

CHANGING POWER of this very simple exercise.

If you haven't followed through with each exercise so far, please go back and complete each success step as outlined. **If you did follow through, CONGRATULA- TIONS!** You need to keep up the good work. **Continue to follow the steps each day**. Make them a regular part of your life.

This book is a practical, step by step strategy for success. I could spend pages and pages giving you stories and examples, philosophies and parables to "prove" that this formula has worked for scores of others. Those things are all well and good, however, my purpose in this book is to give you an immediate strategy to change your life as quickly as possible. There's time for "philosophizing" later on—once your life is running smoothly. NOW is the time for action. The results will speak for themselves.

In each chapter we will ADD a SUCCESS STEP. **Each chapter BUILDS on the other.** That's why it's very important that you have followed the success steps from the previous sections. It's kind of like being in math class. Remember how that was? You had to master each set of skills before you could move to the next. Otherwise, you wouldn't be able to understand and apply the newest skill set. **So please, be sure that you are taking the actions necessary to complete each exercise and that you're CONTINUING to practice each activity every single day!**

Let's recap what we've done so far:

DREAM A LITTLE (OR BIG!) DREAM

1. Make a list of at least **25 DREAMS.** Look at the list often.
2. Create a **DREAM SCENE** by cutting out pictures of your Dreams.
3. Create a **VIVID VISION** of a day in your **ULTIMATE DREAM LIFE.** Read that vision aloud each morning when you rise and in the evening as you retire.

GOAL FOR IT!

4. Choose <u>three or four of your Dreams</u> to begin working on immediately. Make a separate list called **GOALS.**
5. Make several copies of your **GOALS LIST** and look at it throughout your day. Spend <u>at least three minutes</u> every morning picturing yourself already having achieved your Goals.

THE $35,000 IDEA:
YOUR SIX MOST IMPORTANT THINGS TO DO

6. Each evening before you stop working you need to make a **LIST OF THE <u>SIX</u> MOST IMPORTANT THINGS TO DO** the next day.
7. **<u>Prioritize</u>** the **LIST OF SIX** from *<u>most important to least important</u>*.
8. Keep your list with you **ALL DAY** and work through it one thing after another.

Chapter 6
You ARE What You THINK!

Have you ever heard the saying, *"You are what you eat?"* Most people would agree that it's true. People who eat healthy foods and stay away from drugs, alcohol and tobacco tend to be strong and healthy. Their bodies and their health reflect their lifestyle. Wouldn't you agree? Take a walk down the alleys of any major city and look at the homeless people who live on the streets. Their bodies are worn down, they're tired and usually much older looking than their years. Again, their bodies and their appearance reflect their lifestyle.

Well, the mind is no different. What we put into our minds—the things we think about continually, the TV shows we watch, the people we listen to and the "self talk" that we have with ourselves—is reflected in who we are. **Your life today is a direct result of your thoughts up until this moment.** It's true. **YOU ARE WHAT YOU THINK!**

I've given you the STEPS to take... creating a dream list, discovering your purpose, goal setting, etc. **But none of it will result in drastic, long-term change unless YOU CHANGE YOUR THINKING.** Zig Ziglar calls it "Stinking Thinking." It's an epidemic. I see people with this disease (stinking thinking) everywhere—even in my own circle of influence. **Stinking Thinking is more destructive than any "physical" disease I've ever seen—and it's highly contagious.** Are you a carrier?

**If you're going to CHANGE your LIFE
you must first CHANGE your THOUGHTS.**

Your SUCCESS STEP for this chapter is very simple—but not easy. You need to go find a RUBBER BAND. **I want you to wear that rubber band around your wrist every single day for the next month** (you don't have to wear the same rubber band every day. You can change them!)

Every time you find yourself THINKING or SPEAKING something NEGATIVE, I want you to SNAP that rubber band against your wrist. Doing so will help you gain control over your "Stinking Thinking." By snapping the rubber band you will immediately focus your attention elsewhere and be able to redirect your thinking. **By the end of the month you should be well on your way to eliminating the STINKING THINKING from your life!** This exercise, like all of the others, will WORK WONDERS if you will simply practice it every day.

Chapter 7
Accentuate the POSITIVE...
Eliminate the NEGATIVE!

There is nothing more dangerous or destructive than a life of NEGATIVE thinking. Negative attitudes and remarks are the first sign of a "toxic" person. When you meet people who always have "an opinion" (which is never good), who continually make excuses, find fault, place blame and almost rejoice in telling you all the reasons why something "won't work"—you should avoid these people like the plague.

There is nothing "realistic" or "noble" about being negative. These folks will try to convince you that they're just "realists"... they help you keep your feet on the ground and your head out of the clouds. Don't believe them. In fact, take a good hard look at them. What kind of lives are they living? Do they work in careers they love? Are they debt free with plenty of money in the bank? Do they have great relationships with their spouses and children? Are they well respected and admired in their churches and communities? Are they healthy? Do they smile and live with a sense of joy and enthusiasm? I can answer that for you... NO!

These are clearly NOT people that you need to associate with or to allow to influence the decisions you make. If you need advice or encouragement, only seek it from people who are doing BETTER than you are. If you need help with your finances, talk with someone who makes A LOT MORE MONEY than you do. If you need assistance in building a healthier body, only speak with someone who has the kind of body you want to build. But whatever you do, DO NOT allow "DREAM SQUASHERS™"—toxic, negative people—to influence your life.

So, what happens if YOU are the Dream Squasher™? If YOU are the one with the "stinking thinking?" The first thing you need to know is that the kind of thinking that has gotten you where you are today will NOT lead you to where you want to go tomorrow. You will need to go on a mission to eliminate the "negative" from your life—and that begins with YOU!

Our thoughts are an instrument that produce tangible results in our life. What you THINK is what you are. Everything that you have... everything that you are... it ALL begins in your MIND. Your mind is a powerful tool for good or evil. You get to choose.

The Bible says, *"As a man thinks in his heart, so he is."*

The mind is a very complex computer. It was designed to be the tool that would allow us to create and experience anything and everything that we could possibly think or imagine. It has the ability to create something from nothing. It's like a genie in a magic lamp. All we have to do is make the request and it will go to work to manifest each and every result, as we have asked.

The problem is, most people ask for exactly the opposite of what they really want. Your mind—especially your subconscious mind—is extremely efficient. It takes the information, suggestions and emotions that you feed it or allow to be fed to it from others and uses them to manifest your reality.

If you spend your days in worry and fear over what will happen next... How you don't have enough money to pay your bills... How you hate your job and how your boss doesn't like you... How you never have enough time to do anything you want... How your friends always seem to have "more" or "better" than you... How you'll never get ahead... if these are things that occupy your mind, this is the reality you will live.

Remember the television show, "I Dream of Jeannie"? In the beginning of the show Tony (Major Nelson) was constantly making choices or giving commands that Jeannie would immediately fulfill—without realizing he was doing it. His words—which were immediately obeyed to the "letter"—got him in all kinds of trouble. Why? Because he didn't watch his words. He used them recklessly. The commands he made were opposite of the result he wanted to achieve. We all watched, laughing at him, thinking how silly it was. And it was comical. But it was also a very accurate portrayal of what we do on a daily basis.

Our subconscious mind is our "Jeannie." And while we may not see it physically, it is just as powerful as she was to Major Nelson. Our THOUGHTS create our life. Not our circumstances. Not our families. Not our employers. Not our government. Our THOUGHTS are what create the world we live in.

Your mind can ONLY create in reality what you feed it. You CAN'T obsess on problems, shortcomings and "lack" and expect a life of positive, joyful abundance. This is one of those Universal Laws that I told you about. This cannot be changed. What you spend your time thinking about, obsessing on, visualizing for yourself, this WILL be your reality. So, if you want to change your life, simply change your thoughts. You can eliminate anything by simply refusing to think about, worry over it and obsess on it. What we THINK about we BRING about. It's just that simple.

I'm sure you can think of several people (you may not have to look too far) who are close to you that are controlled by their "stinking thinking." They concentrate on the negative side of their everyday existence—seeing only the worst possible outcome in most situations. They expect bad things and that's exactly what they continue to receive. These are the people who others tend to feel sorry for. The people who "never get a break"... who have "all the bad luck"... you know the type.

Remember that I told you that your sub-conscious mind is like a computer. It doesn't discriminate against your dreams and visions. It doesn't know if they're right or wrong for you. It simply takes the commands and goes to work at manifesting them into reality.

You hold the power to change your life completely—in a matter of an "instant." You don't have to live as a victim of circumstance or lack. However, your life will only change when your MIND changes. You must con-

trol your thoughts and guard your mind with tighter security than Fort Knox.

It's important for you to realize the power that you
hold in your hands. YOU can choose the direction in which
your life goes. You can take ANY desire that you have, create a vision for it, determine that you WILL have it and it
WILL come true. It's a powerful tool that you have. You can
use it to create good things or bad—it's totally up to you.

Chapter 8
What You Think About You Bring About

You must guard your mind from negative thoughts and emotions. You are in control of your thoughts. You can put a stop to a negative thought the moment it enters your mind. Is this easy? No, but it is absolutely critical to your ultimate success.

One effective tool for you to use is to REPLACE worry with a positive vision. Worry brings fear, nervousness and frustration. It distracts us and keeps us from operating at our optimum level.

Worry stems from FEAR. And in 90% of all cases, FEAR is negative. Yes, there are times when fear can be healthy—like choosing not to walk too close to the edge of a cliff. But for the most part, FEAR is nothing more than FALSE EVIDENCE APPEARING REAL (F.E.A.R.).

The problem with allowing your mind to obsesses and worry over something you fear is that by doing so you can actually manifest the very thing you fear into your reality. Remember, our subconscious mind works hard to bring about the thoughts we focus on the most.

So here's the plan: when you start to worry over something, instead of doing what most people do and imagining the worst possible scenario as being inevitable, begin to imagine that BEST possible outcome you can think of. Instead of obsessing over "what could or might" happen that is bad, begin to vividly imagine that what WILL happen is a good and positive outcome. If you'll do this, I guarantee that you'll begin to see GOOD things happen and you'll eliminate the bad.

Fear and worry lose their power if you're not willing to play the game. If you're a chronic worrier or live with a lot of fear, making this one change will add years to your life. It doesn't take days, weeks or months to implement. You can make this change this very moment. Simply DECIDE that you will REPLACE fear and worry with a positive vision for the outcome of every situation you face.

You'll have to make a conscious effort to do this. But the more you put your positive outcome practice into place, the more natural it will become for you to choose the bright side in difficult situations.

Another way to eliminate the majority of fear and worry is to practice living in the "NOW." Most people miss out on a large portion of life because they're either stuck in the past... continually reliving hurtful experiences, feeling guilty, remembering all the failure... or they spend their time worrying about what the future holds and what terrible things are headed their way. The truth is, NOW—the PRESENT—is your only point of power. Yesterday is over, it's dead and gone. Tomorrow hasn't happened. Today, this minute, is all you really can depend on. So use this moment to create the life you desire. When your mind starts to wander backwards to the past or forward to the future, stomp your feet on the floor, breathe the air around you and live in the moment.

If you make it a practice of only dealing with problems or challenges that are facing you in the moment, you will eliminate over 95% of all problems and challenges. Most of our problems are either in the past or something imagined that will never happen anyway (unless of course we obsess on them enough to manifest them for ourselves).

Just remember, what you THINK about you BRING about.

Chapter 9
It's All About Faith

At this point on our journey you've established what you WANT in life and created a vision of a day in your ultimate dream life. You've begun eliminating the negative from your life and replacing fear and worry with a positive outcome.

You can SEE what you want. Now you have to BELIVE that you will get it.

It's all about FAITH.

The Bible says,
"Faith is the substance of things hoped for, the evidence of things not seen."

As a Christian I am constantly reminded throughout the Bible that I can have or do anything I believe I can. As a child I was taught to have FAITH that things would always work out for my good. My parents instilled a sense of FAITH in me that has allowed me to move throughout life with a higher degree of confidence and security than most other people I meet.

Faith is the essential building block of your success. It's what stands UNDER your hopes and dreams. It's the foundation of your life.

We ALL have faith. Unfortunately, we do NOT all use our faith for positive, productive outcomes.

The person who goes around saying, "Nothing good ever happens to me"... "If it weren't for bad luck I'd have no luck at all"... "These things just always seem to happen to me"... "I'll never get ahead"... these are statements of FAITH. These people have great faith in what they're saying. They truly believe that "these things just always happen to them." They believe that their life is ordered by a series of unfortunate circumstances. And even worse, they believe that it's totally out of their control—that there's nothing they can do to change it.

This is FAITH. Faith is a strong belief in something. A foundation that you build your life on. If your underlying belief is that nothing good ever happens to you, then guess what? Nothing good will ever happen to you! We GET what we EXPECT. NOT what we WANT. NOT what we HOPE FOR, but what we EXPECT! Our expectations are fueled by our FAITH.

I'm sure you've heard the stories of immigrants who come to America envisioning a land of opportunity and abundance. Within just a short time of arriving here with absolutely nothing, they manage to create fortunes for themselves. Why is this? It's their FAITH. They BELIEVE that America is a land of open arms, pocketbooks and opportunity. They BELIEVE that all they have to have is a dream and the willingness to accept nothing less than what they envision for themselves and their families. They GET what they EXPECT.

So, what kind of FAITH do you have? Is it a high grade of "I can do anything" faith or is it the "poor me, bad things always seem to come my way" kind of thinking?

Think about people like Walt Disney, Oprah Winfrey, Bill Gates, Mary Kay, Robert Schuller, Dave Longaberger and Steven Spielberg.

Not a single one of these people are anything "special" or "extraordinary"—but they ALL have extraordinary FAITH and the ability to BELIEVE they can achieve that which they desire. Where would we be without them? Our lives would be a lot less full. How about you? What great contribution are you depriving the world of because of your faulty faith?

So, how do you begin living with a better level of FAITH?

It's a conscious choice. The truth is, whether you think you can or you think you can't, you're RIGHT! That's a powerful principle in life—and it's absolutely true.

You can change your FAITH and BELIEF in a second. If you're practicing all of the previous steps in our journey... creating a dreams list, determining your purpose in life, creating a vision of a day in your ultimate dream life and eliminating negative people and thinking in your life... you will find that changing your FAITH will be the next logical step.

43

We all have to believe something. Why not choose to believe something good will happen? Why not choose to build your foundation on the rock solid belief that everything in life works according to your good? Living with faith that always sees and expects adversity and hardship is like building your house on sand. The first wave that comes along will wipe you out and leave you with nothing. But when you live life with "possibility thinking"—always expecting the good and positive outcome—you will be prepared to face challenges head on, knowing that they are only temporary and in no way a deterrent to you achieving the life you deserve.

You can't buy faith, you can't be treated for it, there's no pill or magic potion. It's a simple choice and you can make it anytime. It's a gift that God gives us. True faith is like God whispering in your ear and holding your hand through every part of your day. It's a peace that comes from deep within. It's a sense of security knowing that everything will be just fine. It's the starting point from where joy springs forth. It's a simple "knowing" that allows us to live freely, without fear or worry.

As children most of us were blessed to have parents who created a safe and loving environment for us. We were loved and knew that our parents would take care of us. We didn't live in worry or fear—we lived in faith. We saw our parents as giants who protected and provided for us 24 hours a day, 7 days a week, 365 days a year.

The Bible calls it "childlike" faith. Take a few minutes and recall what that was like. We didn't question whether or not things would work out... we didn't play the "what if" game... we didn't worry where the food was coming from or how the bills would be paid. We had FAITH that things would be fine—we didn't know any different.

That's the way we must live our lives as adults. We still have a Father who protects and provides for us every minute of everyday. He's a big strong giant—just like our parents were—who will always make sure that we are safe and that we have what we need.

It's up to you to choose what kind of FAITH you will have. The choice is ONLY yours and you have total control over it. You know what you WANT in life. But you'll only SEE IT when you BELIVEVE IT.

I know that saying all of these things is one thing and actually living it is quite another. I don't pretend that this is easy, but I do believe that if your PRIZE IS CLEAR, the effort you'll have to make to change your thinking and upgrade your faith is but a small price to pay.

Most people are in the habit of speaking and thinking all kinds of negative or limiting words and thoughts. It's an unconscious habit. And to make the changes necessary to live a rich life of abundance, you will nccd to make a conscious choice to create a new habit. You can do it. I know that you can.

Just stop for a moment and think over your dreams list. Think about your vivid vision. Close your eyes and feel what it's like to spend a day in your "ultimate dream life." Let yourself feel the great joy and peace that fills your heart and home.

Now let me ask you... is it worth it? Will you make

45

the extra effort to follow through on these exercises and new courses of action? You will if your prize is clear.

Chapter 10
The Ancient Formula for Success

Understanding the CREATION PROCESS

The information and exercises I've outlined in the previous chapters will allow you to bring about the CHANGE you desire. By following my instructions you can reshape your world and create the life you've always dreamed of.

What I'd like to discuss with you now is the actual PROCESS or FORMULA that is used to CREATE a specific result. As a matter of fact, it's the same process God used to create the world—and everything in it!

The CREATION PROCESS includes various elements from previous chapters—you'll recognize them as you read along. The purpose of sharing it with you is simply to give you a quick, concise example of exactly how to bring about a specific result.

There are certain "immutable" laws that govern the universe. These laws can work FOR you or AGAINST you.

YOU get to decide.

I'm going to share a very simple FOUR STEP CREATION PROCESS using a few of these laws to create WEALTH—or whatever else you want in life. (I just assumed that WEALTH was something that you'd be interested in. If it's not, simply replace WEALTH with whatever you desire when following the exercise.)

There are FOUR STEPS needed to bring about a certain result in life. You should be aware that you're using these FOUR STEPS as we speak. You use them every day. But there's a good chance that you're using them AGAINST yourself to create results that are unpleasant or unfavorable. Nonetheless, these FOUR STEPS represent the CREATION PROCESS and your life today is a result of using this FOUR STEP PROCESS.

Let's look at the steps you'll take to CREATE WEALTH in your life.

STEP ONE... BE

To have wealth you must BE wealthy. Now I know what you're thinking, *"Yeah, that's right. Tell me something I don't know. I don't have wealth because I'm not wealthy."*

The truth is, you can BE anything you choose to be. Today, right this very minute, you can BE wealthy. Just decide. You have a RIGHT to BE wealthy. You CAN be WEALTHY. It's just a matter of a simple decision. So, BE wealthy.

48

Now on to STEP TWO... THINK

This one's a little bit harder. **But remember, your THOUGHTS create your life.** You've been working on these thoughts for some time now. You should be well on your way to eliminating most of your "stinking thinking."

To be wealthy you need to begin to THINK thoughts of wealth. You MUST completely eliminate negative thoughts. As soon as a negative thought creeps up on you—SQUASH IT! Get rid of it right away.

Begin to THINK positive and prosperous thoughts. Don't think about NOT having money or NOT being able to pay your bills or NOT being able to buy something you want. **Instead, think ONLY POSITIVE THOUGHTS**. Imagine every outcome as the best possible scenario. **See yourself with lots of money, with MORE than you need, with financial abundance.** Not tomorrow... not next week... not next year... NOW! **You must see it NOW!**

NOW is the only POINT OF POWER. Yesterday doesn't matter, tomorrow doesn't exist. Only NOW makes any difference. **You can eliminate almost 100% of fear, doubt, worry, anxiety, guilt, etc., if you'll simply REFUSE to live in the PAST or PREDICT THE FUTURE** (as far as the negative things that "could" happen).

NOW is all that matters-it's all there is. Begin to live in the NOW—seeing yourself as BEING wealthy, as HAVING MORE than you could ever want or need. **If you'll do it—barring doubt and negative thoughts—YOU**

49

WILL HAVE IT!

What you THINK about you BRING about. It's absolutely true and cannot be changed. Look at your life today—it's a result of what you THINK ABOUT constantly. **If you want to CHANGE YOUR LIFE you can only do so by CHANGING YOUR THOUGHTS.** So, if you want to BE WEALTHLY, you must begin to THINK as a wealthy person. The results will follow—I know it's true.

Now, on to STEP THREE... SPEAK

Your WORDS are very powerful. They follow your thoughts. Just as with "being" and "thinking", your WORDS can work FOR YOU or AGAINST YOU. **The choice, as always, is YOURS.**

The Bible gives us many great examples of the POWER of WORDS. In Genesis, we witness the first demonstration of the power of WORDS (or the LAW OF COMMAND). God SPOKE the world—and everything in it and on it—into existence. He started with NOTHING and began SPEAKING it into existence.

You must WATCH YOUR WORDS—because just as it is with "thinking"—what you TALK ABOUT, you BRING ABOUT. This is another immutable law. You can't change it, but you can benefit from it if you understand how to use it properly.

You need to begin SPEAKING yourself into wealth. Begin using "I AM" statements. **I AM WEALTHY.** Not "someday I'll be wealthy"... not "I'm going to be wealthy." **I AM WEALTHY—present tense—IN THE NOW!**

50

Pay attention to what you say. **Don't go around speaking yourself poor, sick, unhappy, etc.** Say ONLY positive things. **You can literally change your entire life by simply changing what you think and what you say.**

I take this very seriously. A rule in my company is that everyone MUST have something good to say to every person every time. And no one can walk around saying "we can't" do something or "it's too hard" or "we don't have enough" or "it's not working" or "I just knew (whatever bad thing) was going to or is going to happen." This kind of talk is absolutely forbidden.

WATCH YOUR WORDS. A good way to really get a handle on how you speak is to get a tape recorder and walk around with it for a few days. Tape record everything you say and play it back at the end of the day. You'll be shocked—even while knowing you were being taped—what kind of negative, self-defeating and critical words you use in a day.

CHANGE it right away. **Practice saying very little and not reacting to any news verbally until you can speak POSITIVE, PROSPEROUS outcomes in every situation.**

The last step in the CREATION PROCESS is STEP FOUR... ACT

You're already "BEING" a wealthy person. You're THINKING like a wealthy person and SPEAKING like a wealthy person. **Your last step is to ACT like a wealthy person.**

51

How do you ACT wealthy? It's simple.

Go where wealthy people go. Visit affluent neigh-borhoods. Drive around and pick out your new house. Visit car dealerships and test drive your dream car. Go window shopping in upscale malls or shopping areas. Spend the day in a museum. Rub elbows with other wealthy people.

You don't have to spend money to do this. Wealthy people don't spend every moment of the day spending money. But if you do, spend it with a GENEROUS and GRATEFUL spirit—knowing that you have PLENTY of money for what you want or need.

Any time I begin a new venture or build a new business, I teach the people working with me to "act as if." I tell them this from the very start. That regardless of what our current circumstances may be—let's say we're building a company with a vision for thousands of cus-tomers, but when we first start we may only have a dozen or so customers—we must "ACT AS IF" we were already servicing the thousands.

This is a very important practice to master. It's a nat-ural expression of BEING, THINKING and SPEAKING.

Start right now. **Begin ACTING like the wealthy person that you ARE.** It doesn't matter if your current sur-roundings or circumstances make it appear that you're not wealthy. **If you will BE, THINK, SPEAK and ACT wealthy, YOU ARE WEALTHY.**

That's the CREATION PROCESS in a nutshell. It's a simple process to learn, but it will take some time to do. **You have to really be aware and live in the NOW.** Don't let your mind wander off and create scenes of "lack" or "scarcity." Don't let your words get away from you and speak in negative or scarce terms. And don't act poor.

Wealth is a state of being. <u>As soon as you understand this, you will BE wealthy</u>. This is the reason that a wealthy person can lose all of their money and within just a short time be right back on top. Look at Donald Trump. He has more money today than he did before he lost everything. <u>You can separate a wealthy person from their money—temporarily—but they will always be wealthy</u>. And money or riches is just a by-product of wealth.

The same works in reverse. There are many accounts of poor people coming into large sums of money—winning the lottery, receiving an inheritance, etc. Within just a short time they're back to being poor—many times even worse off than before they received the money. Why? Because they *are* poor. <u>They don't understand the principles of wealth</u>. Even though they may have money, they're still operating like a poor person.

<u>These things I'm sharing with you may or may not make a lot of sense to you, but regardless, I promise you that they're true</u>. **And I guarantee that they'll work for you if you will truly follow my instructions and make the necessary changes.**

In addition to the FOUR STEP CREATION PROCESS, there's one other LAW OF SUCCESS that I would like to share with you...

It's called the Law of Reciprocity.

It's the Law of "Giving."

"As you sow, so shall you also reap."
"Give and it shall be given to you."
"What goes around comes around."

These are all examples of the Law of Reciprocity.

Basically, before you will receive, you must give. You can't change the law. Too many people try to make it work the other way around. They want to GET then GIVE. **Or even worse, they want to only GET.** You can't be a TAKER in a land of GIVERS.

If you really want to see results fast, if you want to be shocked and surprised by how quickly things can turn around for you, **start GIVING.** And I don't necessarily mean only money (although, if it's money you need you should begin "giving it" right away). You can also GIVE your time, talent, expertise, help, friendship, etc.

Generally, the rule is, whatever you want to GET you must first GIVE.

If you want a friend, be a friend. If you want someone to love you, love someone. If you want to grow tomatoes, plant tomato seeds. Get the idea?

If you want to have lots of money, you should be willing to give money. You can start small. It could just be a matter of a dollar to a homeless person standing on a street corner. Or you could pay someone's toll in the car behind you. I'm not talking about big bucks here, it's just important that you become a GIVER.

There's a LAW OF SUCCESS that many people overlook, yet it's been used for centuries. **It's called tithing.** Basically, the concept is that the first 10% of your income belongs to God. Whether you're a "religious" person or not, I encourage you to give tithing a try. The results that have been experienced from this one small idea are absolutely incredible.

**Mark Victor Hansen says,
"A tithe is not a debt we owe but a seed we sow!"**

Some of the richest people of our time used tithing as a cornerstone of their success philosophy. People like Andrew Carnegie, Napolean Hill, W. Clement Stone, Henry Ford and John D. Rockefeller—to name just a few—understood this age old principle and it served them well.

"Give and it shall be given unto you; good measure, pressed down, and shaken together, and running over, shall men give into your bosom. For with the same measure that you measure, with it shall be measured to you again."—Luke 6:38

I encourage you to try it for three months—on a "trial" basis. Give 10% of your income—right off the top— as your tithe. If you don't belong to a church presently, choose one and send them the check. Look for a church that teaches prosperity principles and bless them with your tithe. What you'll receive in return will amaze you. (If you'd like to receive my special report entitled "Giving Your Way to Riches" you can contact my office at 1-877-462-5448 or

55

visit us online at www.InspirationPoint.net)

When you really start using this law to your advantage you will create a snowball effect like you've never seen. <u>The more you give of yourself, your time, your money, your love, your friendship, etc., the more things coming pouring back in your life in much greater measure</u>. And once it starts it's almost impossible to stop.

My whole life I heard my father (who was a preacher) say, "You can't out give God." And you know what, he was absolutely right!

Chapter 11
Step Out of the Boat

The title of this book, *When You Can Walk on Water Why Take the Boat?*, exemplifies the life that most people settle for, verses the life that we have available to us. There's safety "inside the boat"... you don't worry about getting wet or drowning, however, it's outside the boat—on the water—where life really begins. We were created with the ability to achieve extraordinary results in life.

How do we step out of the boat and start achieving extraordinary results?

I have a simple plan for you to follow that will allow you to begin creating a brand new life full of the dreams and visions that you have established for yourself. If you will follow my lead in putting the principles in this book into practice, you WILL witness even your most impossible dreams come true!

While studying "success" and personal development over the last decade, I've researched the lives and accomplishments of many ordinary people who have achieved extraordinary things in life. From Mary Kay Ash and Dr. Robert Schuller to Oprah Winfrey and Walt Disney, these "ordinary turned extraordinary" people have all followed the same principles of success. As a matter of fact, in almost 100% of the success stories that I have researched, I've been able to identify the same core set of principles or strategies that these individuals used in achieving success. And although these people cover the spectrum of accomplishment... from presidents to parents... business owners to athletes... authors to actors... the strategies remain the same.

I've already shared many of them with you in this book. Each exercise that you completed was an important principle in your overall strategy for success. Let's review them again and be sure that you are ready to put them into action.

Step One: **KNOW WHAT YOU WANT**
Your DREAMS LIST will help you identify the things you want to have, do or be in life.

Step Two: **DISCOVER YOUR PURPOSE**
You need to identify the one compelling force in your life. The thing that draws you to it and makes you feel the most happy and fulfilled as a person.

Step Three: **CREATE A VISION OF YOUR DREAM LIFE**
Writing the "Day in your ultimate dream life" movie script will help you create a clear vision for your future. You need to know exactly what to expect from your life, both now and in the future. The more detailed you can be in describing your life, the more easily it will be accomplished. This area will be a continuing work in progress. As you begin to

change your reality and manifest the new life you desire, you'll also continue to write bigger and better things for your future. Keep your vision clear, fresh and current.

Step Four: GOAL FOR IT
Put your GOALS in writing. Anyone can eat an elephant- one bite at a time. Your goals are the sports car that will take you on the fast lane to success.

Step Five: ELIMINATE THE NEGATIVE
This is a big one for people. You must eliminate the negative people from your life—at least eliminate their influence on you. You must also eliminate YOUR negativity. Put an end to "stinking thinking" forever!

Step Six: REPLACE FEAR & WORRY WITH POSITVE OUTCOMES
Put an end to the devastating grip of fear and worry in your life. CHOOSE to imagine the best possible outcome in any situation. FOCUS on what you WANT—not what you DON'T want. When you play the "what if" game, ONLY allow the possibilities to be positive!

Step Seven: UPGRADE YOUR "FAITH"
Remember, we all have to believe something. Choose to believe something GOOD will happen in every situation. Live with expectancy—anticipating only wonderful blessings.

Step Eight: MIRACLE MOMENTS
It's the times when you are consciously putting these principles into ACTION and beginning to create the reality that you deserve that you are experiencing MIRACLE MOMENTS. These are moments of faith, of dreaming "God

59

size" dreams—instead of little "baby aspirations."

These simple steps outlined in this book provide you with the tools you need to CHANGE YOUR LIFE. It may seem like a MIRACLE when it happens—but I assure you that the outcome is as predictable as planting tomato seeds and later harvesting giant red tomatoes.

Chapter 12
Your MIRACLE MOMENTS are Waiting for You Now!

W hen Peter asked Jesus to allow him to step out of the boat and join him by walking on the water, THAT WAS A MIRACLE MOMENT.

In those few short moments, Peter taught us a lesson that holds within it the SECRET to all success in life.

Let's look at what happened.

Peter saw Jesus standing out on the lake. He thought it was totally cool that Jesus could do that and he wanted to do it, too. (He KNEW what he wanted!)

I imagine that, in the few moments preceding his request to Jesus, Peter envisioned himself walking across the lake. He could see himself standing out there next to Jesus—defying all sense of reality or what was "possible." (He created a VISION in his mind.)

When he asked Jesus to call him over there, he was making a bold statement of FAITH. He believed that it was possible.

At the same time I imagine that the other guys in the boat with Peter had a few remarks to make of their own (even if they were made quietly). Peter chose to ignore the NEGATIVE and envision the POSITIVE OUTCOME.

So, what happened? Peter stepped out of the boat, started walking on the water and within a short time, sank.

I wish that weren't what happened. I wish Peter would have walked across the water all the way over where Jesus was standing and then just stood there on the lake and had a chat. But that's not how the story goes. Why did Peter sink?

He knew what he wanted, he created a vision, he had faith that is was possible, he ignored the negative remarks of his buddies and he sank. What's the deal with that?

Within every failure lies the seed of an equivalent success. Peter lost his focus for the moment and instead became overwhelmed with the "reality" of what was going on. He was WALKING ON WATER! People don't do that. It's just not possible, right?

Peter wasn't perfect—neither are we. Things happen. We get off track. We lose sight of the prize and we fail. But, failure isn't bad. It's just a necessary step to success. Nothing ventured, nothing gained. Think about it for a minute. Who would you rather have been? Peter or one of the guys in the boat? Me—I'd rather have a few minutes of doing the impossible than a lifetime of nothing special.

The truth is, YOU CAN HAVE ABSOLUTELY ANYTHING YOU WANT IN LIFE. The secret to achieving extraordinary results are contained within these pages. All you have to do is LOOK for them. If you're READY, you will FIND them.

Chapter 13
MIRACLE MOMENTS

**Success doesn't happen by CHANCE,
it happens by CHANGE.**

The key to creating the new life you truly desire is to put these principles and strategies into DAILY PRACTICE. It's not good enough to simply read this book, think about it from time to time and wait for "miracles" to happen. You have to take ACTION... you have to CHANGE what you're doing now and you have to do it EVERY DAY!

**This daily action is what I call
MIRACLE MOMENTS.**

To develop any new practice or habit it's proven that you need to CONSCIOUSLY do it for at least thirty days. Taking the principles and strategies in this book and immediately incorporating them into your daily life will be easier for some than others. So to make sure that EVERYONE can do this successfully, I've created a simple action plan for you to follow for AT LEAST the next thirty days. (I'm asking you to give it a try for the next three months.)

Each day you will spend a total of **THIRTY MINUTES** making a concentrated effort to work on your new life. Here's how it works...

You will spend five minutes in the morning reading over your DREAMS LIST and vividly imagining what your new life looks like. You will SEE yourself driving the car of your dreams, living in the home of your dreams, doing the work of your dreams with the people of your dreams. **You will end your day by spending five minutes reading your DREAMS LIST and five minutes drifting off to sleep "visioning" your new life in as much detail as possible.** (Talk about sweet dreams—you'll sleep like a baby!)

You will also spend fifteen minutes at some time in your day reading or listening to a book or tape that provides additional motivation and inspiration for your journey of personal development. Turn your car into a mobile classroom. (If you'd like to obtain a copy of my personal list of "required reading/listening" from my own Success Library, you can contact my office at 1-877-462-5448 or visit us online at www.InspirationPoint.net)

It's very important to feed your mind with positive, productive messages every day. These books and tapes will help reinforce your new way of thinking and offer you encouragement to stay true to your vision of a brand new life.

I also recommend creating several positive affirmations or **"STATEMENTS OF FAITH"** that you will repeat to yourself again and again. Affirmations utilize one of the "universal laws" of success, **THE LAW OF COMMAND.** Your words are very powerful. Your affirmations should be specific to what you want.

I've designed a very special audio program that you may be interested in. We custom design an affirmation audio for you to listen to throughout the day. The audio program speaks affirmations to you over and over again—based on the SPECIFIC VISION you have for your life. This audio cassette could literally transform your life in 30 days. For more information, contact my office or visit us online at www.inspirationpoint.net.

If you will faithfully do this for the next month—without exception—you will see a MAJOR TRANSFORMATION in your life in just thirty days—I GUARANTEE IT!

Are you game? It's simple to do and your success is guaranteed!

Chapter 14
Do You Know the Secret?

**You Can Have Anything You Truly Desire in Life
IF You Know the Secret!**

We've spent our time together in this book laying a foundation that will serve you well for the rest of your life. <u>Of course, this is true ONLY if you have taken my training seriously and are practicing the art of successful living each and every day</u>.

If you haven't done the exercises... if you're not putting what you've learned into practice everyday, then you're cheating yourself out of the life-changing results (and rewards!) that are a natural byproduct of following the instruction you've been given.

If you've failed to follow the program—it's not too late! You can still go back and start again. Start with the first lesson and work your way through. <u>Believe me, it's one of the best investments you could ever make</u>. Spend the time to follow my advice and reap rich rewards.

**Your THOUGHTS Create Your Life...
that is the SECRET!**

It sounds too simple—too "elementary" of an idea. But it's true. **Your THOUGHTS really do create your LIFE.** You can have, do or be anything you truly believe you can. **Whether you think you CAN or you think you CAN'T—you're right!**

Don't underestimate the POWER you hold with this fundamental truth. The Bible says, *"All things are possible to him that believes."* **ALL THINGS.** Not just some things, not just "religious" things—ALL THINGS. Do you realize how incredibly powerful that is? Do you understand what a sense of freedom and limitless potential this Universal Law gives you?

ALL THINGS ARE POSSIBLE!

Do YOU believe? That's the KEY. It's in YOUR hands. **You can have it ALL—if you BELIEVE you can.** The fact is, you'll get in life exactly what you EXPECT and what you're willing to ACCEPT. No more, no less. So, take a good look at your life. You'll immediately see the level of your beliefs and the quality of your thoughts.

Success Doesn't Happen by CHANCE...
it Happens by CHANGE!

You can't sit around waiting to "see what happens." Life is not a spectator sport. **If you want big things**—wealth, peace, happiness, plenty, freedom, love, friendships—**you've got to EXPECT big things,** you've got to **CREATE your world FIRST in your THOUGHTS**—only then will your LIFE follow suit.

YOU CAN DO IT! You can make the CHANGES

necessary to create a life of absolute and total abundance. You've got the tools and techniques—I've given them to you in this book. And you've always had the most important ingredient—YOU—YOUR THINKING.

Why not start NOW! Make a commitment to yourself to CHANGE YOUR WORLD BY CHANGING YOUR THOUGHTS.

I know it's not easy or automatic—but consider the alternative. **With "stinking thinking" (negative thoughts) you end up unhappy and unfilled, with a mediocre lifestyle (at best) and no ability to experience all of the abundance and blessings that you were created for.** You'll work long and hard for little—little time, little money, little happiness and little respect. You don't want to live a little life, do you?

This is your moment. TODAY, RIGHT NOW, is your point of power. Yesterday doesn't matter and tomorrow doesn't exist. RIGHT NOW is all that matters. **BE HERE NOW.** That's the key to eliminating fear and worry and MAXIMING every moment of your life. If NOW is all there is—no yesterday and no tomorrow—then NOW is all you have to be concerned with. Most people are so busy living in the past and worrying about the future that they miss out on the only critical time in life—NOW.

**Change your THINKING and you will
CHANGE YOUR LIFE.
It's that simple.**

71

As a Reminder...

THINK POSITIVE THOUGHTS.

Imagine the very best outcome possible in every situation. When you have fear or worry—replace it with FAITH. Imagine good things—not bad. Zap those negative thoughts. Don't let them hang around between your ears—not even for a moment. (Remember, the "rubber band" method will help you get a handle on that "stinking thinking.")

What you THINK ABOUT you BRING ABOUT. So be careful! Have a clear vision for your life. **Know what you want and keep that picture clear in your mind.** Spend your time visualizing yourself living those dreams. Don't daydream negative scenarios. Don't replay past hurts or bad events. Create a "movie trailer" in your mind of what your life is going to be like and see yourself living the life of your design.

WATCH YOUR WORDS.

Speak only positive things. If you can't say something good, say nothing at all. **Add the phrase, *"As you wish,"* behind every sentence you say.** Think about it. When you're complaining, saying things like, "I always have to struggle"... "Things never work out for me"... "It's always the other people who get the breaks in life"... "I'll never have what I really want"... add the words, **"AS YOU WISH"** at the end of those statements.

When we speak negative things we bring them to us. Your subconscious mind doesn't know the difference between good or bad, real or imagined events. But what your subconscious mind does know is that YOU are not a liar. It works hard to fulfill your statements and your thoughts. **It's like your own personal little "genie"—saying "As you wish" to all of your commands.**

WHAT ARE YOU WISHING FOR?

If you want a better life, simply make it a point to have better thoughts and speak better words. It really is as simple as that. When you speak, use commands and statements that will bring you CLOSER to what you want—not further away. Speak in positive, uplifting terms. Your WORDS cause all sorts of "unseen" events and actions on your behalf. **What you say is what you get—so be sure it's what you want!**

GIVE, GIVE, GIVE!

The greatest Universal Law of all is about GIVING. **You will simply NEVER achieve the success or abundance in life that is waiting for you until you become a "GIVER."**

This is not a theory or an opinion of mine. This is a UNIVERSAL, IMMUTABLE LAW. **You must GIVE in order to RECEIVE.**

Some of the richest people ever to live understood this principle the very best. **In the Bible it's called TITHING.** You need to tithe of your TIME, MONEY and TALENTS. **If you're looking to get RICH you must DEFINITELY tithe of your MONEY.**

73

Give 10% of your income—preferably to your church or place of worship. If you don't go to a church, find one (or someone in need) and send them a check. By simply following this principle you will see an increase in your income and your needs will be supplied.

Try it. I guarantee you'll see results. **You simply cannot afford NOT to give.** And it's when you're at the lowest point in life—financially, emotionally, spiritually, physically-that you need to give the very most. So, don't put it off until you have more money. **GIVE and it shall be GIVEN to you.**

If you want to get RICH. If you want to be HAPPY. If you want to have PEACE & PLENTY... FOLLOW THESE PRINCIPLES.

Your success is absolutely GURANTEED—if you follow my instruction. **There's NO LIMIT to what you can HAVE, DO or BE.** You KNOW the SECRET. **Now use it!** May God richly bless you in all that you do!

In closing I'd like to make a request of you...

I'd like to hear from you a month from now, after you've put the principles you've learned into practice. I'd like to share in your success and the incredible results you've experienced. So please, drop me a note, send me a fax, an email or pick up the phone and give me a call. I'd love to hear from you.

"My wish for you and your future is happiness, prosperity and abundant good. My continued thought for you shall be for your prosperity."

About the Author

Lisa Diane is the Founder and Chief "Inspiration" Officer of Inspiration Point—a personal success company whose mission is to encourage, empower and inspire people to realize their potential and live their dreams.

Lisa Diane lost her first business in the early 90s and was left with no income, her car was repossessed, her home was on the brink of foreclosure and her credit was ruined. Her bank account was in the negative and she had over $50,000 in credit card debt.

From there Lisa Diane made some very real and life-changing discoveries that set the stage for a dramatic transformation in not only her own life, but in the lives of countless others around the country. Within about six months of losing her business Lisa Diane started a little direct response marketing business from home—earning over $653,000. Within a year, she grew that little home business into a multi-million dollar company which has generated over $10 million dollars income—all starting from scratch.

In addition to growing several multi-million dollar companies from the ground up, Lisa Diane has experienced stellar success in the network marketing industry. She created a trademarked sales and recruiting system that allowed her to claim the coveted #1 recruiter position out of several hundred thousand distributors, starting in her first month with the company—a position that she maintained throughout her 18 month association. Her powerful system afforded her a $30,000.00 commission check in her first month. But what's most unique and unusual is that Lisa Diane achieved this level of success without any of the "typical" business building techniques—such as personal selling, "one-on-ones", PBRs, conference calls, etc. Lisa Diane's trademarked system teaches ordinary people how to be extraordinary network marketers.

Often called "The Queen of Dreams"—Lisa Diane believes in dreaming your life and living your dreams! She lives in Florida, in a multi-million dollar, tropical island-like, four story waterfront home. Her home was recently featured in a trendy lifestyle magazine

75

as the "Ultimate Utopian Waterfront Estate"—complete with lushly landscaped grounds, an island tiki bar, swimming pool with waterfall, Jacuzzi, steam room, large real wood dry heat sauna, elevator that serves all floors, a gourmet kitchen that would make any chef envious and a 4th story, all glass creative suite that offers 360 degree panoramic views of the Gulf of Mexico.

Lisa Diane provides business consulting, success coaching and training to small business owners, entrepreneurs, network marketers and direct sales consultants around the world. She's a dynamic keynote speaker and an expert on empowerment and results-driven success strategies. Whether you're looking for the inspiration of a good book or audio training, a new business idea or insight or to discover the key to achieving your biggest dreams, Lisa Diane is the person to call.

For more information on Lisa Diane's other products, programs or services, contact her office directly at the following:

Phone: 1-877-GOAL-4-IT ● Fax: 1-800-738-1025
Web Site: www.InspirationPoint.net
Email: Support@InspirationPoint.net
207 South Disston Avenue ● Tarpon Springs, FL 34689